HANDWRITTEN FROM THE HEART

HANDWRITTEN FROM THE HEART

yinyang

Contents

foreword

hi,

this book somehow made it into your hands
and I'm so grateful that you have taken the time to read my words.

this is my first published poetry book —
a compilation of poems that I wrote from ages 15 to 19.

they are not in chronological order; instead, they are pieced together
by the underlying emotion that inspired the poem.

you are about to take a journey through my deepest, most vulnerable thoughts and emotions that I translated into poetry throughout my teenage years...

I hope that you find yourself in a poem, which will help you wherever you are in life right now.

this poetry book is very much about the heartbreaks and aches of adolescence as much as it is about the beauty and magic of it.

if you are a teenager reading this,

I promise you: everything that you're experiencing right now is shaping you into the person you are meant to become.

and for the record, that person is pretty amazing.

GRATEFUL PEOPLE
TODAY, I AM GRATEFUL FOR...
TODAY I AM GRATEFUL FOR
grat·i·tude
noun
a mental tool that makes happiness a way of life

if you don't have control over your mind
then what power do you really have?
change your mind and change your world
HAND ♡
in gratful
for Being A kind
girl - margaret
in gratful
for frends

longing

*"Sometimes you have to travel a long way
to find what is near."*

Paul Coelho

it's funny.
it so often feels as if I am trapped
in a one-sided glass cage.
I can see everything
I can hear everything
yet no one can hear nor see me
I am technically there,
but not really.

I am a hopeless romantic
I have never been in love,
but I believe in it anyway

my heart yearns for someone
who really knows me...
who is at least for now,
unknown to me

- late night thoughts from a soul deprived of a much needed love
story

we are all too well trained by society
to hide our great fiery souls
under a great façade of ordinary.

FOMO mantra:

12/31/18

you are exactly where you need to be in this very moment

everyone is on their own path

all experiences you need to experience will come to you

when the time is right

I'm not searching for a fairytale anymore
just another soul
that ignites the fire in mine

                          look
                   I don't need a man

to be happy
or find fulfillment
or even love myself

my soul is very much content
                              thank you

it is simply
the yearning
to find someone
to daydream about
when I listen to a love song

she rolled her eyes
at clichés in movies
maybe because
she had seen them a thousand times
or maybe because
all she really wanted
was one of her own

    - a secret romantic hypocrite

am I in love with you?
or just the person that you were before?

MYLONELYSOULISSCREAMINGFORANOTHER-
LONELYSOUL

being single at 17

being single at seventeen
is the tiny pings of butterflies in your heart
not due to excitement or giddiness
but the painful reminder
that others have someone
and you don't.

being single at seventeen
is hearing all the love stories, songs, and movies
of falling in love with others
and not being one of them.

being single at seventeen
is the broken promise of society
who told you
that you would find love by seventeen.

it's the desperation of wanting to find love
of wanting to be loved
that has been accumulating
ever since the ability to understand love
yet being helpless
in the attraction of it

being single at seventeen

feels like an unbreakable curse
I want to break free
but I can't.

infatuated

*"Wherever you are, whatever you do,
be in love."*

Rumi

the thought
of being drowned
by the smell of him
by the sound of his laugh
by his ocean blue eyes
didn't terrify her —
and that's when she knew —
the infatuation was real

I would say that you completely swept me off my feet
but it only took one look from you
and I was already on the ground

     - I didn't need any help   for you
                            falling

I must admit
that I'm rarely paying attention
to the words you're saying
I really am sorry
but the fantasies of adventures
and dreams of far-off lands & magic
never stop playing in my mind...

nothing lasts forever
but in this moment
it kinda seems
like you & I will

ocean waves

morning birds

a campire

an afternoon rainstorm

the city at night

honestly,
I'd choose your voice
over them all

- every single one of my senses is captivated by you

how is it
that having a crush
is simultaneously
wonderful
fantastic,
heartbreaking,
terrible,
yet absolutely
magical?

the hopeless romantic in me
thinks that it's absolutely terrifying
that I am head   in love with you
                    over heels

the cynic in me thinks
that it's even more terrifying
that maybe it's all just infatuation

but the me that I am with you
knows the most terrifying part
is that it really doesn't matter

                             dance with me

barefoot
in the middle of the street
under a rainstorm
                                sing with me

late at night
windows rolled down
and volume all the way up
walk with me
along the streets of Paris
or
an imagined version of it
because while our hearts are full,
out bank accounts
are not
                                run with me

through a field of flowers
on a cloudless summer day
where we can pretend
that we are boundless
and infinite
                                lay with me

beneath a sky full of stars
making wishes on the first one we see
but knowing
that this moment
is all we could ever want

honestly
I don't care what we do
as long as I'm with you

a love letter to rain

I find it absolutely incomprehensible
why anyone
would want to carry an umbrella
when they could carry
intoxicating kisses
on their skin
or why one would prefer
to wear raincoats
when they could experience
your warm puddles of love
beneath their feet

there is something
quite magical
about you
there's a dazzling element in your ways
that sunshine simply
does not have

but
I would walk through
a thousand sunny days

if it meant
I could spend
just one
dancing with you

so, Rain
a billion "thank you's"
could never quite cover
my gratitude
for your mere existence
but I thank you
not only for bringing wonder
to my world
but the entire world

you are a magnificent miracle of hope

how silly it was
for her to think
that no one could ever love her
with the way he was looking at her
right now

yours lips are too irresistible
to not dream about kissing them

roses
command attention
with their dripping red costumes of allure
and captivating perfume

tulips
delight the hills come springtime
crowning fresh greenery in pastels

sunflowers
arch towards the heavens
majestically looming beneath the clouds

daises delight in white
carnations pepper public gardens
lilacs flirt with lazy summer breezes

and all eyes are on them
in the joyous golden daylight

when night falls
and the energetic exuberance
of it all dies down
there lies veiled patches of white
birthed by the moonlight

tucked beneath the shadows of trees
and bushes of leaves:
the moonflowers

unbeknownst they may be
their beauty is as beautiful as beauty can be
possibly even more so —
with no one else around to see.

10/05/21

and suddenly
I was one of those teenagers
drunk on the night air
and high on hormones
walking beneath the city lights
with a giddy smile & disoriented thoughts
hand in hand
with a boy who might break my heart
but filled it so completely in the moment
kissing
at a table placed just for us
unaware and uncaring
of other people passing by
hot breath
on my neck
fist full of hair
hands
everywhere
suddenly I was one of those teenagers
and I happily did not care

12/03/21

I don't know
but when it's just him and I
nothing else in the world could possibly matter

you're making me overthink
like no one else has before
I'm losing my mind
at the mere thought
of you & I
and living
in absolute
fear
that we're going to break each other's hearts
again.

- *in too deep*

wait —
feelings weren't supposed to happen
I never intended for it to get this far
just friends at the start
now here we are

I've never felt so loved and unworthy
all at the same time
can you see what you're doing to me?
and now I can't think.

now it's getting hard to breathe
and you're absolutely infuriating
always so calm, collected, and cool
… who knows it too

please don't ever become someone I lose

you now occupy a space in my mind

and now I only dream of you

1/1/22

loving you is the discreet
smile that I can't help
with your body against mine
when it's only you and I
and your fingers gently
brushing against mine
is enough to make me
want to
collect all of the stars
that aligned
for us to be together
in this moment
and float amongst them
eternally

you are a manifestation
of my dreams
with strings attached
strings that I am already
bound to
that I constantly contemplate
whether to cut them
or become a knot

you are my first love
though you may not be
truly mine,
my daydreams cast you as otherwise

and while what we have
may be criticized,
it can't compromise
the stars that dance between our eyes
or the infinity that exists
when our hands are intertwined

loving you
is everything I've ever hoped
I'd find

1/07/22

there is something so beautiful
about young love
the way both souls can be
simultaneously brimming with life
and so delicately intertwined

how the eyes sparkle
with absolute infatuation
in such reckless nature

always in pursuit of the next adventure
and not giving a damn
about the worries of the future

you are someone I let walk
through the door

you are the someone I couldn't keep my guard up against anymore

you are someone I have allowed
swirl through my mind
and interrupt my thoughts
ravage my plans
give love a second chance

you are someone
I've explored in the dark
made you feel the spark
and now we both might
break each other's hearts

but despite my hesitations,
in spite of the complications,
no matter the odds or what
the world says about who we are,
I cannot ignore
the feeling of being in your arms
or the fact that you're everything
I've ever dreamed about and more

- you are my someone

and now we're simply in too deep
to allow the rain to wash away
all the memories we've made.

there's no denying that they're ingrained
in permanent memory
tattoos on your heart
the kind that will either
light you up
or haunt you in the dark

everything
from the moment
that you walked in late
to late nights in your embrace

you didn't have to ask me
for a ride to the station
and it didn't have to lead you
to meeting me at one later

I know that you can still feel
the goosebumps laced on your skin
from the picnic we had at the beach
on a 60 degree day
and the way they stuck around
when you accidentally called it a date

it's a delicate work of art
the high we were flying on
as we stumbled through the dark

drunk on whiskey and
the excitement of something really being there
I dare you to live
one-hundred lifetimes to try
and find something that rare

there's no doubt it'll forever
echo   through your mind
the first time your lips were on mine
and how we lost all track of time

try as you may
but it will be on
continuous replay
the heat on your face
from the Korean chicken we ate
and the kind that we made later that day
lying in the park
or parked in my car

and it will just be too hard
to forget
being in your room
just us two
feeling like nothing else really matters
'cause I'm here with you

ode to my lust to wander

my soul aches to explore places
I've never visited before

it yearns to see the world
and leap across the shores
-
finding new adventures
learning different cultures
seeing things with fresh eyes

this is all I could ever want
in a lifetime

- this and nothing more

with you,
drowning feels easy

and when the end of the road is dead,
when all the lights are red
even when all of the signs surrounding you
scream "Don't Go Ahead!"
she would voyage further in a heartbeat
if it meant she could see him again

she was the gardener
he was the storm
and together
they watered a flower
that couldn't grow

disillusioned

"No feeling is final."

Rainer Maria Wilke

08/26/21

the feeling of utter embarrassment is never as bad
as the feeling of utter regret.

I went to the airport today
looking for a destination, an escape
but
there were no tickets
to the place where I most wanted to be

- the warmth from your arms still haunts me

all of the girls

I hope you fulfill your needs
with all of the other girls
I hope you're happy with them, too
I hope you're sleeping good
next to her
I hope she wakes up feeling
safe in your arms

hopefully
you never notice the bitterness laced
in my voice
or my emotionless face as you tell me
that you'll be with her tonight

let's hope
you never see my jealousy
eating away the good memories
that you and I made
when it was only you and I

let's hope you'll always believe I'm fine
when I'm dying inside
and that my smiles are real
on the outside

she deserves someone like you
but I deserve more.

9/24/22

if it doesn't feel like your heart
is being stabbed, is it love?

if tears aren't running down your face
does a relationship mean anything at all?

if what you have doesn't feel torturous ,
what else is there to feel at all?

maybe, sometimes I think,
I like the pain and suffering
of falling off a cliff in which
I know there's nothing that will
save me at the bottom

maybe, I like to break
my own heart

but that's better than someone else doing it for you.

I hate the way you've made me
insane.

I hate the way you've stolen
my heart
and now it's no longer mind

I hate the way you've convinced me
with your charisma and
cheeky charm
and stupid grin and laugh

I hate the way you've hijacked my brain
and driven my train of thoughts
around a loop of
never-ending you

I hate the way you whisper my name
and how it melts my heart completely

and I hate the way your arms wrap perfectly around my frame
and make me feel safe

I hate the way we laugh together
and make fun of each other
and go to new places

and now now every time I get
a notification on my phone
I cling to the sad hope that it's you

I hate the way you showed your love for me
because I've fallen for you
and I hate admitting that it's true

11/20/21

to love someone that is not truly yours
and will never be only yours
feels like a haunting state of euphoria
it is a kind of pain that you never let through the door, though it sits
there on the porch
the kisses are passionate
the love between you two is real —
but it is never enough to make it feel whole
it's wanting with every part of your soul
to want to believe him
when he says
that you are everything
that he is looking for
but you know
the truth that you try
so hard to ignore
is still there
and you know it
from deep within your bones.

- can't I just kiss you without feeling like second place?

10/05/22

forced smiles and helpless ones
flickers of hope and shots in the dark
addictive pain and torturous hurt

making room for confusion and not clarity

you snuck your way into the walls of my heart
I want to call the guards,
but I can't

I feel like I'm living on Cloud 9
that isn't mine
but I'll happily borrow it
temporarily

10/07/22

how did you turn me not giving you
a second thought
into you consuming them all?

I'm not the type to fall fast
but I'm the type to fall deep.

now you got me holding my breath
every time my phone rings

and you broke my heart once
too many times
for it to still sting
when I see that it's not your name.

congratulations:
you've stolen my heart, my mind, and my highest hopes

so now instead of wishing for you,
all I want is to have me back.

I hate waiting in this pool of my
overflowing thoughts
and second-guessing

I'm getting tired of being tied to
this string that keeps pulling me
in the direction of you

it's unfair that I'm sitting here lost
in my mind on the verge of losing it
while you're MIA without a care

I wish my more conscious, logical self would take the lead
because I'm sick of sitting on the sidelines

I'm sick of feeling that you're the only person I want to talk to,
sick of being consumed by the urge to check what you're up to

why can't you just text me back?

lost

"At the center of your being you have the answer; you know who you are and what you want."

Lao Tzu

stop wishing on stars
and start chasing them

just because you can't foresee your destination,
doesn't mean your journey isn't beautiful —
that's exactly where the beauty exists

9/22/21

let the sky fill your heart
it's okay to feel whole,
even if the world around you is not.

let it sparkle inside of you —
and smile —
you don't need a reason to.

inexplicable happiness
is like overhearing a harmonic song
floating on the wind past your cheek:
follow it before the wind gets windier.

you don't have to make rain
to stop & admire rainbows.

just like sunsets are beautiful because
they are beautiful,
joy should be appreciated
because it is joy.

stop trying to understand why flowers grow,
or worry if someone may step on them,
and just admire the garden before you

sit back,
allow existing things
to simply
exist.

- that includes you too

my heart is a melodic sirens' song
thump, thump, thump
it beckons me forward

though I can't always see them,
the stars remind me
I never walk alone

and the celestial dust
that runs through them
serves as a reminder
that every step is never in vain.

deep in the core of my being,
my soul pulsates
its glow leads the way

a light whose shine
never fades.

N
W
E
S

7/04/22

more than anything,
you deserve your dreams.

the glowing burn in your belly
is hunger that is meant to be satiated.

do not ignore the aches in your heart
or pangs in your soul

you must leap off of the ledge
no matter how much opposition
stands in your way.

drift with the wind that whispers in your ear
allow it to carry you to your heart's desires

from there, only look back to see
how far you've come

don't worry about the destination
because dreams are always about
the detours and personal development
that happens along the way.

you deserve your dreams,

more than anything.

I think you're so brave for crying.

I think when water cascades down your face
it shows the purest form
of human emotion —
it doesn't always mean sadness.

it doesn't detract from your worth.

your tears are the battle scars
from showing up fully in life

a celebration of vulnerability
turmoil transformed into peace

so I hope that you are never ashamed to cry.

it's simply a reminder that you're human
and will soon be on your way to thrive

10/20/22

and when your emotions flow through you
like an ocean
know that it's okay
and that the magnitude of your feelings
is nothing to run from,
but to celebrate

there's such a powerful strength that you possess
that manifests most clearly
in these moments —
own it.

this state of vulnerability
is a reinforcing reminder
of just how beautiful you are
when it's just you and you own heart

you don't have to be a ray of sunshine all of the time

you are not a burden
just because the emotions you're
wearing on your sleeves aren't yellow

it's called being human —
and you never have to apologize for it

11/14/22

listen to you heart
it's beating just for you

feel your chest ride
and use your breath as your guide

stop for a moment
and admire your smile
it's lighting up the world
that you've created for yourself

you should be beyond proud
because look how far you've come
from the start of it

promise me
that you won't lose sight of your dreams
you've got so much ahead to see

and all the while
rest assured that
your glow will only burn brighter
and the currently obscure path
will become a lot lighter

maybe it's okay
to stand frozen at forks in the road
to be completely blind in your footsteps
to not know where to go
or where you're going
to feel defeated when trees block the path
and alone as you tip-toe around them.

it's okay
to be overflowing with sunshine
only for it to turn into grey,
to walk through the darkness
without knowing why,
to be skeptical yet hopeful
that everything will be
okay.

for what it's worth
it is okay
to not always
be okay;

it is valid to feel alone though you
have someone

it is normal for the world to feel so
overwhelming that you just want to run

and it is brave
that you persist anyway.

enchanted

"Allow yourself to experience every note that the heart can play."

- Michael A. Singer

11/16/19

I'm so thankful
to simply be a part
of this beautiful planet called Earth
where the sky turns pink
and water comes down from the sky
and birds sing and there's laughter and love and heartbreak
I'm so grateful for this life I've been given

- late night thoughts

because
I guess when you look at it this way...

why search
and dream
of magic
in a far-off land
when darling,
you live in a world
that is illuminated
by a giant ball of fire in outer space
which then lights up a Mercury-sized rock at night

in a world
where the sky turns random shades
of pinks, purples & gold
for absolutely no reason at all
and the occasional water show
erupts down
providing life for all

and sometimes,
after the raindrops,
a faint pastel ribbon of various colors
looms over the trees...
the literal representation of hope

- who ever said there was no such thing as magic?

sometimes
I wish that
the morning
was infinite
and other times
I wish that some nights were

I guess you can say
I'm an imposter morning person
who loves the night

10/14/19

standing out there
just me & the rain
my legs were numb
and I couldn't feel my face
but my soul was warm
so I was okay.

- *forever in love with rainstorms*

the sea

expansive
it seems; a never-ending eternity
scintillating
it sparkles; mirroring a glow like no other
tranquil
it breathes; a meditative pattern that calms me
tumultuous
it can become; a hurricane-like passion you can't outrun
mysterious
it is; a treasure trove of secrets that will never be told
majestic
it will forever be; a beautiful complexity known as the sea

it's truly extraordinary
to find beauty
in the most ordinary of things

nineteen in NYC

nineteen in NYC
was a dream
a liberating one
the kind where a young girl
finds independence
and freedom rides in the wind
that glides through the skyscrapers
and the city lights
electrify the eyes
the hustle and bustle
invigorates your bones
nineteen in NYC
carefree, still a teen —
maybe slightly naive —
and a whole world left to see

NEW YORKER

Narrow Road to the Interior

"I do not know when it first began,
but enticed by a cloud wafting in the wind,
my desire for wandering has never ceased."

- Matsuo Bashō

spring haiku trilogy

rain cascading down
cherry blossom petals fall
evanescent spring

grey overcast skies
magnifying the birds' song
mellifluous trees

rebirth of fresh green
splashes of pink around me
cool air and puddles

never go too long
without watching a sunset

thought tornados

"Look at you, worrying so much about things you can't change...
You'll spend your whole life singing the blues
If you keep thinking that way."

Taylor Swift, "Starlight"

09/05/22

a willow tree sits on the shore, hanging parallel over the water
it's branches bend, one or two kiss the surface
I ponder: is it hanging on for dear life or is it trying to dive in headfirst?
it is still and the morning is peaceful.
with absolutely no resistance, the willow tree is simply existing
perhaps neither, I conclude.

09/01/22

do you like me or do you like the image I like to project
it's easy to fall for me when it's all based on illusions
and ill-fated reciprocities
when you touch me
is there a spark or just the sensation of my skin
I repeat to myself:
never fall when there's no love
but that doesn't stop me from daydreaming of you
get too close to me—
and I promise,
you'll dream of me too

09/27/22

my volatile heart
bursts at the seams
at every mere thought of you
waves of blue cascade from head to toe
because I miss you.
maybe I should get my hormones checked,
because I've never felt so off balance in my entire life
it's infatuation that's borderline insanity
how did I get this way?
because the water is creeping up over my head
and the only sound I can hear is your name

6/14/21

you dream of fantasies and far-off places

but look around you

this is it

you're living in one

and if you don't stop to notice

you'll miss

                        the magic that's all around you

hopeful

"You must live in the present, launch yourself on every wave, find your eternity in each moment.
Fools stand on their island of opportunities and look toward another land.
There is no other land; there is no other life but this."

Henry David Thoreau

I don't think there's anything more comforting
than the reassurance that the sun will rise in the morning.

The inevitability that comes with light overcoming darkness
no matter what
is why I will always have hope.

the arrival of spring

as the cold days of solitude
gradually melt
into blue skies, bird chatter, and efflorescence
a glorious breath of relief is released
drifting into the winds of change
of peaceful change
and transformation
hues of ebullience
peak through
wishing to bask in the long-waited rays of warmth
and hope
the Earth awakens from its monochrome world
and for the first time in a while,
feels free

in the blink of an eye,
daydreams turn into reality
longing morphs into butterflies
and your feet finally become still

fantasies that are more spectacular
than you could ever see or believe

I don't think
there is a more comforting thing
than the reassurance
that the Sun will rise in the morning

the inevitability of the light overcoming the darkness no matter
what...
I hope the thought fills you
with as much hope
as it does for me

pronoia:

the opposite of paranoia;
the feeling that the world is conspiring good for you

in spite of everything —
somewhere within the long, lazy days
of the realm of nostalgia & innocence
her heart is still swinging on the swings of her childhood
either high on the sky on a cloud
or
singing in the forest with the fairies

while her mind moved out long ago (as most minds do)
from the peer pressure
and antagonization from societal norms
her heart still swings, swings, swings

not disillusioned
just not willing to give up
the feeling of freedom in a fantasy

- you may teach her responsibilities,
but she will never give up on her dreams
of possibilities

if you can train your mind
to believe in magic
you can train your eyes
to see it

- there's magic in the ordinary too

being single at 18

being single at eighteen
feels like a "happily ever after"
with a plot twist

into the daylight I walk
holding nothing
but my head high
and the assured peace
that comes from outgrowing a pipe dream
that clouded my head
with longing for something
I didn't need to have

yes,
the moon is beautiful
but I prefer to be a self-illuminated star
alone in the night sky —
yet never truly alone

blank pages

just waiting to be filled
waiting to occupy space
and take up ink

what stories will be told?
what words will be written?

it is a mystery.

until the end,
it's unclear when chapters will proceed
into the next
or which ones
you liked best
and how every single one of them
serves a meaningful purpose
that you may at first miss...

p.s.

a letter to my teenage self

11/23/22

Dear whoever needs to hear this:

if life suddenly became a nicely paved path for you to follow with a brightly-colored ribbon, I hope you'd be concerned you walked onto a movie set.

Because the truth is, life doesn't always present itself with clarity.

Really, it never does because what lies ahead is simply not within our control.

And whoever said that life is even a path?

I'd like to argue that it's more comparable to a hiking trail with no path, signage, or even a clear indication of where it leads.

The road to the unknown.

And guess what?

Everyone is on it.

Sure, some may have the fancy hiking equipment that appears to make navigation easier — but that doesn't change the reality that it's impossible to tell what truly lies ahead.

Life's journey is one that is inexplicably beautiful and tumultuous and intensely emotional.

It's filled with people and places who touch our souls, fill our hearts and expand our minds.

Life is also unpredictable, volatile, and ever-changing.

We spend our entire lives living without ever unlocking life's "master plan."

Because we aren't supposed to.

And so it's okay — more than okay — to feel as if you're going through life blindly.

You may not have it all figured out right now or ever.

That doesn't mean your life isn't as beautiful; on the contrary, the mystery of it all magnifies life's magic.

And while many in society will not accept this truth, I really hope that you're someone who can embrace it.

This life is yours and only yours to live.

Stare the unknown in the face and dare to embark on your dreams.

No matter how risky it seems or how loud your limiting beliefs are.

Do it now without knowing, or risk never knowing.

with love,
20-Year-Old Me